THIS GUIDE BELONGS TO

_____

AS THEY PARENT

_____

Date / Year

_____

Kind Words

Kind Words from Parents, Grandparents, & Experts in Parenting

Sandra Stanley
Author of *Breathing Room*, and co-author of *Parenting: Getting it Right*, foster care advocate, mother of three

We all know where we want to end up in our parenting, but how to get there can seem like an unsolved mystery. The *Phase Guides* give us a resource to help out. They help to guide parents and caregivers through the different seasons of raising children, and provide a road map to parenting in such a way that we finish up with very few regrets.

ENDORSEMENTS

Sissy Goff M.Ed., LPC-MHSP
Co-director of Child and Adolescent Counseling at Daystar Counseling Ministries, speaker and author of 12 books, including *Brave*

It's hard to connect with your child without first understanding where they are. As counselors and speakers at parenting events across the country, we spend a great deal of time teaching parents about development. To know where your child is—not just physically, but emotionally, socially, and spiritually, helps you to truly know and understand who your child is. And that understanding is the key to connecting.

The *Phase Guides* give you the tools to do just that. Through the research of the Phase Project, *Phase Guides* are an insightful, hopeful, practical, and literal year-by-year guide that will help you to understand and connect with your child at every age.

Jennifer Walker, RN BSN
Author and co-founder of Moms On Call, mother of three

These resources for parents are fantastically empowering, absolute in their simplicity, and completely doable in every way. The hard work that has gone into the Phase Project will echo through the next generation of children in powerful ways.

Tina Naidoo
Executive Director of The Potter's House of Dallas, Inc

It's true that parenting is one of life's greatest joys but it is not without its challenges. If we're honest, parenting can sometimes feel like trying to choreograph a dance to an ever-changing beat. It can be clumsy and riddled with well-meaning missteps. If parenting is a dance, this *Phase Guide* is a skilled instructor refining your technique and helping you move gracefully to a steady beat.

For those of us who love to plan ahead, this guide will help you anticipate what's to come so you can be poised and ready to embrace the moments you want to enjoy.

Kind Words

Carlos Whittaker
Speaker, storyteller, best-selling author of multiple books, including *How to Human*, father of three

Not only are the *Phase Guides* the most creative and well-thought-out guides to parenting I have ever encountered, these books are essential to my daily parenting.

With three kids of my own, I know what it's like to swim in the wake of daily drama and delicacy. These books are a reminder to enjoy every second. Because it's just a phase.

Cheryl Jackson
Founder of Minnie's Food Pantry, award-winning philanthropist, grandmother

As the founder of Minnie's Food Pantry, I see thousands of people each month with children who will benefit from the advice, guidance, and nuggets of information on how to celebrate and understand the phases of their child's life.

Too often we feel like we're losing our mind when sweet little Johnny starts to change his behavior into a person we do not know. I can't wait to start implementing the principles of these books with my clients to remind them… it's just a phase.

David Thomas, LMSW
Co-director of Family Counseling, Daystar Counseling Ministries, speaker, and author of 10 Books including *Wild Things: The Art of Nurturing Boys*, father of three

I began exploring this resource with my counselor hat on, thinking how valuable this will be for the many parents I spend time with in my office. I ended up taking my counselor hat off and putting on my parent hat. Then I kept thinking about friends who are teachers, coaches, youth pastors, and children's ministers, who would want this in their hands.

What a valuable resource the Orange team has given us to better understand and care for the kids and adolescents we love. I look forward to sharing it broadly.

ENDORSEMENTS

Josh Shipp
Best-selling author of *The Grown-Up's Guide to Teenage Humans*, award-winning speaker, teen expert, father of three

As I speak to high school students and their parents, I always wonder to myself: What would it have been like if they had better seen what was coming next? What if they had a guide that would tell them what to expect and how to be ready? What if they could anticipate what is predictable about the high school years before they actually hit?

These *Phase Guides* give a parent that kind of preparation so they can have a plan when they need it most.

Danielle Strickland
Speaker, global social activist, author of *The Other Side of Hope*, mother of three

The *Phase Guides* are incredibly creative, well researched, and filled with inspirational actions for everyday life. Each age-specific guide is catalytic for equipping parents to lead and love their kids as they grow up.

I'm blown away and deeply encouraged by the content and by its creators. I highly recommend Phase resources for all parents, teachers, and influencers of children. This is the stuff that challenges us and changes our world. Get them. Read them. And use them!

Courtney DeFeo
Author of *Treasured* and *In This House* and *We Will Giggle*, podcaster, mother of two

I have always wished someone would hand me a manual for parenting. Well, the *Phase Guides* are more than what I wished for. They guide, inspire, and challenge me as a parent—while giving me incredible insight into my children at each age and phase. Our family will be using these every year!

Parenting Your Four-Year-Old

A GUIDE TO MAKING THE MOST OF THE "WHY?" PHASE

THE PHASE PROJECT

Parenting Your Four-Year-Old:
A Guide to Making the Most of the
"Why?" Phase

Published by Orange, a division of The reThink Group, Inc.,
5870 Charlotte Lane, Suite 300, Cumming, GA 30040 U.S.A.

Parent Cue ® is a registered trademark of The reThink Group, Inc.
It's Just a Phase ® is a registered trademark of The Phase Project, LLC.

All rights reserved. Except for brief excerpts for review purposes,
no part of this book may be reproduced or used in any form without
written permission from the publisher.

ISBN: 978-1-63570-217-0
© 2024 The Phase Project, LLC

Printed in United States of America
Second Edition 2024
1 2 3 4 5 6 7 8 9 10
06/01/2024

Special thanks to —

JON ACUFF for guidance and consultation on having conversations about technological responsibility

JIM BURNS, PH.D for guidance and consultation on having conversations about sexual integrity

JEAN SUMNER, MD for guidance and consultation on having conversations about healthy habits

CHINWÉ WILLIAMS, PH.D for guidance and consultation on how to navigate crisis

Every educator, counselor, community leader, and researcher who invested in the Phase Project

In Partnership →

Parent Cue partners with the Phase Project, designing Phase Guides to help you parent your child through every year in the four main phases: Preschool, Elementary School, Middle School, and High School.

The Phase Project →

Started in 2013, the Phase Project is a synthesis of personal experience, academic research, and gatherings of leaders and educational experts from across the child development spectrum.

Contents

How to Use This Guide 12

Welcome to a New Phase 14

1. 52 Weeks to Parent Your Four-Year-Old 16
- **MEASURE** *Your Weeks* 20
- **DISCOVER** *This Phase* 28
- **MILESTONE** *First Days of Preschool* 38

2. Six Things Every Kid Needs 42
- **LOVE** *One Question Your Four-Year-Old Is Asking* 48
- **STORIES** *Books to Read to Your Four-Year-Old* 54
- **WORK** *Work Your Four-Year-Old Can Do* 60
- **FUN** *Ways to Have Fun with Your Four-Year-Old* 66
- **PEOPLE** *Adults Who Might Influence Your Four-Year-Old* 72
- **WORDS** *Words Your Four-Year-Old Needs to Hear* 78

3. Four Conversations to Have in this Phase 86
- **HEALTH** *Establish Basic Nutrition* 90
- **SEX** *Introduce Them to Their Body* 96
- **TECHNOLOGY** *Enjoy the Advantages* 102
- **FAITH** *Incite Their Sense of Wonder* 108

4. Rhythms and Responses 114
- **CUE TIMES** *Building Daily Rhythms* 116
- **UNEXPECTED** *Preparing for the Unexpected* 122
- **CRISIS** *Navigating Crisis* 126

5. What's Next 130
- **SUMMARY** *The Kindergarten Phase* 134
- **TIMELINE** *The Preschool Phase* 136
- **NOTES** *Write and Remember* 140

Parenting Your Four-Year-Old

How to Use This Guide

The guide you hold in your hand doesn't have very many words, but it does have a lot of ideas.

Some of these ideas come from thousands of hours of research. Others come from parents, educators, and volunteers who spend every day with kids the same age as yours. This guide won't tell you everything about your kid, but it will tell you a few things about kids at this age.

The best way to use this guide is to take what these pages tell you about four-year-olds and combine it with what you know is true about your four-year-old.

After each idea in this guide, there are pages with a few questions designed to prompt you to think about your kid, your family, and yourself as a parent. The only guarantee we give to parents who use this guide is this: You will mess up some things as a parent this year. Actually, that's a guarantee to every parent, regardless. But you, you picked up this book!

You want to be a better parent. And that's what we hope this guide will do: help you parent your preschooler just a little better, simply because you paused to consider a few ideas that can help you make the most of this phase.

INTRODUCTION

Let's sum it up:

Things about four-year-olds

Thoughts about your four-year-old

Your guide to the next 52 weeks of parenting

Parenting Your Four-Year-Old

Dear Parent,

Welcome to a new phase!

WHO *REALLY* KNOWS what provokes that mischievous glint in the eye of a four-year-old just moments before they deliver the kick that makes the block tower tumble? I suspect it's something about the thrill of destruction combined with the wondrous spectacle of discovery. Four-year-olds blend the reckless abandon of toddlerhood with the wide-eyed glimmer of preschool learning. You don't have to look very closely to see the wheels turning in that still-disproportionately-large head of theirs. They're taking in

INTRODUCTION

everything they possibly can about the big world around them, categorizing things, naming things, and putting it all together like a puzzle.

But the world of a preschooler is much more complex than the average puzzle. Every time your four-year-old learns something new, they will immediately discover three more things they never thought to ask before. Life is a maze of questions and answers that lead to more questions.

As a preschool leader at a church preschool, I still remember the day I was tasked with teaching the Ten Commandments. An especially advanced four-year-old child who could read our handout asked me what "adultery" meant. Caught off guard, I replied, "It has the word 'adult' in it, and when you are one, you'll understand."

Four-year-olds are notorious for asking questions that are hard to answer in four-year-old terms. Most parents of four-year-olds find themselves at one point or another stumbling through long, winding, well-intentioned explanations about things they aren't even sure they know how to answer in adult terms.

But don't overthink their curiosity. Most preschoolers will remember the reaction on your face and the tone of your voice far longer than they will the accuracy of your words. It's okay to leave some questions unanswered. Or, better yet, to only give the shortest, simplest answer possible. But just remember, the most extraordinary privilege is simply to connect to the heart of the four-year-old who is looking to you to guide them on their journey of discovery. We are, as exhausted explainers of every variety, quite beautifully, the first voice that gets to show the way.

Maybe that's what makes the four-year-old year the most incredible year for establishing a solid foundation in your preschooler's heart and mind. You are their first teacher. You are setting the tone for the elementary school years. So use this year to engage their wonder and imagination. Allow yourself a few minutes each week to get into their world and see through their eyes. Listen and learn alongside them. Let their curiosity remind you to ask a few questions about life that maybe you haven't considered in a very long time.

Jennifer Walker, RN BSN

Pediatric nurse, mother of three, toddler consultant, author and co-founder of MomsOnCall.com

52 Weeks to Parent Your Four-Year-Old

MEASURE *Your Weeks* 20
DISCOVER *This Phase* 28
MILESTONE *First Days of Preschool* 38

WHEN YOU SEE HOW MUCH TIME YOU HAVE LEFT, YOU TEND TO DO MORE WITH THE TIME YOU HAVE NOW.

There are approximately 936 weeks from the time a baby is born until they grow up and move to whatever is next.

SECTION 1.   MEASURE

It may seem hard to believe, but <u>at least 208 of those weeks have already passed you by</u>. And, while things like giving your kid a cell phone, taking pictures before prom, or sending them off to college still feel far away, you're probably beginning to realize that your kid is growing up faster than you ever dreamed.

That's why every week counts. Of course, each week on its own might not feel significant. There may be weeks this year when all you feel like you accomplished was simply not falling to pieces when you saw just how many toys are now in your living room. That's okay.

Take a deep breath. You don't have to get everything done this week.

But what happens in your child's life week after week, year after year, adds up over time. So, it might be a good idea to put a number to your weeks.

Measure It Out

HINT:

If you want a little help counting it out, you can download the free Parent Cue app on all mobile platforms.

Write down the number of weeks that have already passed since your four-year-old was born. Then write down the number of weeks you have left before they graduate high school.

Write down the number.

Create a Visual Countdown

Find a jar and fill it with one marble for each week you have remaining with your child. Then make a habit of removing one marble every week as a reminder to make the most of your time.

Where can you place your visual countdown so you will see it frequently?

SECTION 1.　　MEASURE

Which day of the week is best for you to remove a marble?

_____
_____
_____

Is there anything you want to do each week as you remove a marble?

HINT:
Say a prayer, write in a baby book, retell one favorite memory from this past week.

Bonus idea—place the marble you removed into a second jar so you can see how much time you've invested in your child.

23

Parenting Your Four-Year-Old

You only have 52 weeks with your four-year-old while they are still four.

Then they will be five, and you will never know them as a four-year-old again. That might be incredibly emotional, or it might be the best news you've heard all day.

Or to say it another way:

> Before you know it, preschooler will grow up a little more and…
> → learn to ride a bike.
> → tie their own shoe.
> → wash and rinse their own hair.

Just remember, the phase you are in now has remarkable potential. Before their fifth birthday, there are some distinctive opportunities you don't want to miss.

So, as you count down the next 52 weeks, pay attention to what makes these weeks different from the rest of the weeks you will have with your child as they grow.

SECTION 1.   MEASURE

EVERY PHASE IS A TIMEFRAME IN A KID OR TEENAGER'S LIFE WHEN YOU CAN LEVERAGE DISTINCTIVE OPPORTUNITIES TO INFLUENCE THEIR FUTURE.

Reflect

What are some things you have noticed about your four-year-old in this phase that you really enjoy?

SECTION 1.   MEASURE

What is something new you are learning as a parent during this phase?

The phase when anything can be imagined, everything can be a game, and one curious preschooler wants to know, "Why?"

SECTION 1.   DISCOVER

Imagination is reality.
Your four-year-old's delightful imagination may suddenly turn your bedroom into a train station, a castle, or both. But imagination may also turn deceptive. Your four-year-old may suddenly insist the cat ate her cupcake, her bed somehow got wet from the rain, and maybe it was Grandma who spilled nail polish on the furniture.

Everything can be a game.
You motivate your preschooler best when you appeal to their desire to play. Whatever the task, turn it into a game; make it fun. You might even let them take the lead and create a game you both can play. Your four-year-old is wired to have fun with you.

They have a newfound curiosity.
Whether it's showcased by pouring all the dish soap into the sink at once, or the constant repetition of "Why? Why? Why?", your preschooler is eager to know how the world works. So when they ask you "Why" for the second and third time, remember they're just looking for more of the knowledge they know you must have as an adult person.

Parenting Your Four-Year-Old

Every four-year-old is unique.

Even with unique four-year-old—which yours most certainly is—most four-year-olds have a few things in common. This book will show you what those are so you can make the most of the "Why" Phase.

Remember: We haven't met <u>your</u> four-year-old. This book is just about a lot of four-year-olds.

SECTION 1. DISCOVER

Some can recite the Bible story word for word Sunday afternoon

Some will belt their favorite song note for note every. Single. Day.

Some draw people with two to four body parts.

Some draw people with anatomically correct body parts.

Some can dress themselves.

Some will only dress as a superhero with a cape.

Some take turns willingly.

Some take tantrums seriously.

Some think their preschool teacher hangs the moon.

Some think preschool is a prison sentence of three hours to life.

Some use scissors to cut out paper snowflakes.

Some use scissors to cut their hair.

Some complete 50-piece puzzles.

Some are puzzles. (Okay, that's all of them.)

Parenting Your Four-Year-Old

This year, your four-year-old is changing.

Physically

① Hops on one foot

② Strings beads and cuts with scissors (the plastic kind)

③ Throws a ball overhand and catches a bounced ball (sometimes)

④ Draws circles, squares, and a person with 2-4 body parts

Mentally

① Sorts things and ideas into categories

② Recognizes "less" and "more" (especially if it's candy)

③ Can argue, explain, and rationalize (you may have noticed)

④ Lives in the present, but enjoys retelling the story of past events

SECTION 1.   DISCOVER

Verbally

1. Tells a short story
2. Keeps a conversation going
3. May struggle with some sounds: r, l, s, z, j, sh, ch, th
4. Adjusts speech based on the listener and location

Emotionally

1. Tends to be optimistic in spite of failure
2. Enjoys both physical humor and simple jokes
3. Can learn relaxation techniques (take a deep breath)
4. Often deals with fear and anxiety by distracting themselves

Parenting Your Four-Year-Old

What are some changes you are noticing in your four-year-old?

You may disagree with some of the characteristics we've shared about four-year-olds. That's because every four-year-old is unique.

What makes your four-year-old different from four-year-olds in general?

SECTION 1.   DISCOVER

What do you want to remember about this year with your four-year-old?

HINT:
There are enough lines for at least one per week. Throughout the year, write down a few simple things you want to remember.

Parenting Your Four-Year-Old

SECTION 1. DISCOVER

… *Parenting Your Four-Year-Old*

First Days of Preschool

SECTION 4. MILESTONE

Big changes can come with big feelings—for both you and your child. If your child is going to preschool this year, here are a few ways to help them adjust:

Talk about what to expect. Tour the school and meet the teacher before the first day.

Develop skills for managing stress. Practice deep, slow breathing. Say phrases that encourage resilience like, "I can do hard things."

Set clear morning and evening routines. Consistent routines help your child feel secure and confident.

Get enough sleep. It's normal if your child is cranky at the end of the day. Find time for rest after school, and prioritize an early bedtime.

Remind your child to ask for help. The teacher wants kids to ask for help when they don't understand something, need to use the restroom, or need a drink of water.

Reflect

What is one word to describe how you feel about your child attending preschool?

What is your biggest concern about your child going to preschool this year?

SECTION 1.   MILESTONE

Since you know your kid better than anyone, what are some unique ways you can build their confidence to do something new and scary?

Six Things Every Kid Needs

LOVE *One Question Your Four-Year-Old Is Asking* **48**
STORIES *Books to Read to Your Four-Year-Old* **54**
WORK *Work Your Four-Year-Old Can Do* **60**
FUN *Ways to Have Fun with Your Four-Year-Old* **66**
PEOPLE *Adults Who Might Influence Your Four-Year-Old* ...**72**
WORDS *Words Your Four-Year-Old Needs to Hear* **78**

Parenting Your Four-Year-Old

WHEN YOU SEE HOW MUCH TIME YOU HAVE LEFT, YOU TEND TO MAKE WHAT MATTERS, MATTER MORE.

SECTION 2. SIX THINGS

It's worth repeating: When you see how much time you have left, you tend to make what matters, matter more.

Depending on your personality, that can sound empowering, or just like a lot of pressure. Relax. Every day doesn't have to create a memory worth posting.

The important thing to remember is a countdown clock doesn't mean you try to squeeze more things into each week so you can get the most out of it. It actually means acknowledging that you can't do what you can't do.

You can't make your preschooler always behave in public. But over time you can show them the kind of love that is the foundation for how we treat each other.

You can't make your preschooler make wise choices. But over time you can introduce them to stories that widen their perspective and inform their decision-making.

You can't make your preschooler be a good friend. But you can give them safe places to belong so they will know that people matter.

You can't make your preschooler perform at the top of their class. But you can make learning fun, and use mistakes as opportunities to grow.

This week matters because it's an opportunity to give your preschooler a few things that really matter. You can't do what you can't do. Let some things go, and you might just discover you're already doing more significant things than you ever realized.

Parenting Your Four-Year-Old

Your kid needs six things over time.

Over the next 728 weeks, your child will need many things.

Some of the things your kid needs will change from phase to phase, but there are six things that every kid needs at every phase. In fact, these things may be the most important things you give your kid—other than food. Kids need food.

The next few pages are designed to help you think about how you can give these things to your four-year-old—before they turn five.

SECTION 2.   SIX THINGS

Every kid, at every phase, needs:

 Love to give them a sense of *worth*.

 Stories to give them a bigger *perspective*.

 Work to give them *purpose*.

 Fun to give them *connection*.

 People to give them *belonging*.

 Words to give them *direction*.

Parenting Your Four-Year-Old

No. 1

Every kid needs **love** over time to give them a sense of **worth.**

SECTION 2.   LOVE

One question your four-year-old is asking:

Life for your four-year-old can be confusing. It's okay to throw a ball, but not a rock. You can hug your friend, but not squeeze his neck. Your four-year-old is learning the rules for life and probably encountering some necessary discipline. Your four-year-old is asking one major question: **"Am I okay?"**

Your preschooler needs to know you love them—even when they make bad choices. As the parent of a four-year-old, who may test your limits on a daily (or hourly) basis, you may feel overwhelmed at times. But remember this—in order to give your four-year-old the love and discipline they need, you need to do one thing: **Embrace their physical needs.**

> When you embrace your four-year-old's physical needs, you...
> ① communicate that they are safe,
> ② establish that the world can be trusted, and
> ③ demonstrate that they are worth loving.

Reflect

You are probably doing more than you realize to show your four-year-old just how much you love them.

Make a list of the ways you already show up consistently to embrace your four-year-old's physical needs.

HINT:
You may need to look at this list on a bad day to remember what a great parent you are.

Showing love requires paying attention to what someone likes.

What does your four-year-old seem to enjoy the most right now?

It's impossible to love anyone with the relentless effort a four-year-old demands unless you have a little time for yourself.

What can you do to refuel each week so you are able to give your four-year-old the love they need?

SECTION 2.   LOVE

Who do you have around you supporting you this year?

No. 2

Every kid needs **stories** over time to give them a bigger **perspective.**

Books to read with your four-year-old:

Mae Among the Stars
by Roda Ahmed

Feelings
by Aliki

Stellaluna
by Janell Cannon

Corduroy (*series*)
by Don Freeman

Pete the Cat (*series*)
by Eric Litwin and James Dean

A Morning with Grandpa
by Sylvia Liu

The Hueys in the New Sweater
by Oliver Jeffers

Stuck
by Oliver Jeffers

Make Way for Ducklings
by Robert McCloskey

Princess Hair
by Sharee Miller

Thank You, Omu!
by Oge Mora

It's Okay to Make Mistakes
by Todd Parr

You Matter
by Christian Robinson

We Are Grateful: Otsaliheliga
by Traci Sorell

Gerald and Piggie (*series*)
by Mo Willems

A Chair for My Mother
by Vera B. Williams

The Little Mouse, the Red Ripe Strawberry, and the Big Hungry Bear
by Don and Audrey Wood

HINT:
You can find a more in-depth reading list at ParentCue.org.

Reflect

Kids need the kind of stories you will read to them over time. But they also need family stories.

HINT:
Remember to look at this list throughout the year to continue to capture your family's story.

What can you do this year to capture your family's story so you can retell the story of this year to your four-year-old when they are older?

SECTION 2. STORIES

What makes your family history unique? How can you preserve the story of your family's history for your four-year-old?

Are there other stories that matter to you? What are they, and how will you share those stories with your preschooler?

SECTION 2. STORIES

Parenting Your Four-Year-Old

No. 3

Every kid needs **work** over time to give them **purpose.**

SECTION 2.   WORK

Work your four-year-old can do:

- Dress themselves
- Write their first name
- Make simple snacks
- Sort toys and put them away
- Sort laundry *(darks / lights)*
- Dust large surfaces
- Help set the table *(napkins and flatware)*
- Put dishes in the dishwasher
- Help put detergent in the dishwasher
- Hang up wet towels *(hang a hook on their level)*
- Help carry groceries *(the light ones)*

Reflect

What are some things your four-year-old has worked to accomplish so far?

SECTION 2. WORK

How are you giving your four-year-old opportunities to help out at home? What do you do to reward their efforts?

Parenting Your Four-Year-Old

What are some things you hope your four-year-old will be able to do independently in the next phase?

How are you helping your four-year-old develop those skills now?

No. 4

Every kid needs **fun** over time to give them **connection.**

SECTION 2. FUN

Ways to have fun with your four-year-old:

● Games
● Activities

- Candyland®
- Swing together
- Alphabet letters
- Painting (Finger paints, watercolors)
- Hungry Hungry Hippos®
- Crayons
- Chutes and Ladders®
- 24-piece puzzles
- Don't Break the Ice®
- Throw or kick a ball
- Play-Doh®
- Cootie®
- Ants in the Pants®
- Don't Spill the Beans®
- Play "Duck, Duck, Goose"
- Play freeze games
- Play "Simon Says"
- Memory®

Reflect

What are some activities that make you and your four-year-old laugh?

SECTION 2. FUN

When are the best times of the day, or week, for you to set aside to have fun with your four-year-old?

What are some ways you want to celebrate the special days coming up this year?

Fifth Birthday

Holidays

No. 5

Every kid needs **people** over time to give them **belonging.**

SECTION 2.   PEOPLE

Adults who might influence your four-year-old:

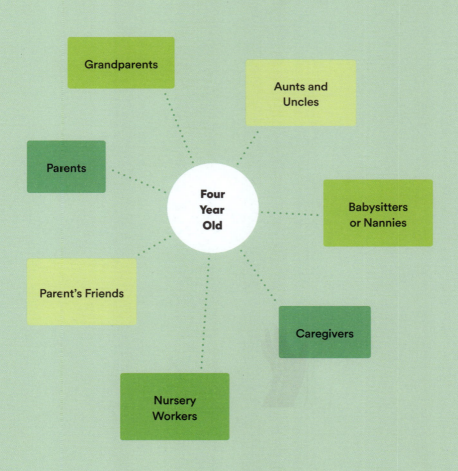

Reflect

HINT:
They're probably the adults your four-year-old talks about.

List at least five adults who have influence in your four-year-old's life right now.

SECTION 2.   PEOPLE

What is one way these adults could help you and your four-year-old this year?

EXAMPLES:
Pray for you, take your four-year-old to the library, give advice to help you get ready for kindergarten

Parenting Your Four-Year-Old

What are a few ways you could show these adults appreciation for the significant role they play in your child's life?

SECTION 2. PEOPLE

No. 6

Every kid needs **words** over time to give them **direction.**

SECTION 2.   WORDS

Words your four-year-old needs to hear:

- I love you!
- You're okay.
- Good morning!
- Keep trying.
- Thank you.
- Please.
- You can do it.
- You're welcome.
- I will be back.
- I'm sorry.
- Good night!

The best way to begin preparing your four-year-old for school is by improving their vocabulary. Here are a few suggestions:

① Talk to your preschooler—the more, the better.
② When they talk, make eye contact.
③ Give your preschooler opportunities to make choices.
④ Read, sing, or make up rhymes.
⑤ Join your child in pretend play.

Reflect

What word (or words) describe your hopes for your four-year-old in this phase?

Determined	Motivated	Gentle
Encouraging	Introspective	Passionate
Self-Assured	Enthusiastic	Patient
Assertive	Joyful	Forgiving
Daring	Entertaining	Creative
Insightful	Independent	Witty
Compassionate	Observant	Ambitious
Amiable	Sensitive	Helpful
Easy-Going	Endearing	Authentic
Diligent	Adventurous	Inventive
Proactive	Honest	Devoted
Optimistic	Curious	Genuine
Fearless	Dependable	Attentive
Affectionate	Generous	Harmonious
Courageous	Committed	Empathetic
Cautious	Responsible	Courageous
Devoted	Trustworthy	Flexible
Inquisitive	Thoughtful	Careful
Patient	Loyal	Nurturing
Open-minded	Kind	Reliable

SECTION 2. WORDS

Where can you place those words in your home so they will remind you what you want for your four-year-old this year?

Don't be surprised if you find yourself wanting to text your four-year-old's comments to a friend—it's simply too good not to share.

Just make sure to go back and write it down somewhere more permanent than your phone (like here, on this page). The words of your four-year-old can become the stuff of great family stories for years to come.

SECTION 2. WORDS

WHEN YOU SEE HOW MUCH TIME YOU HAVE LEFT, YOU TEND TO VALUE WHAT HAPPENS OVER TIME.

SECTION 2.   SIX THINGS

The most important things we give our kids aren't the gifts we just give once, but the ones we give over time. Just remember...

We don't experience worth because we are loved once, but because we are **loved** by someone over time.

We don't understand the world through a single event, but through a collection of **stories** over time.

We don't usually discover our purpose in one great revelation, but through consistent opportunities to **work** over time.

We don't develop trusted relationships in a day, but we become connected to others through laughter, **fun**, and shared experiences over time.

We don't know we belong because of a single invitation, but because we have been welcomed by **people** over time.

We are not motivated to action by one statement, but by **words** that move us over time.

Four Conversations to Have in this Phase

HEALTH *Establish Basic Nutrition* 90
SEX *Introduce Them to Their Body* 96
TECHNOLOGY *Enjoy the Advantages* 102
FAITH *Incite Their Sense of Wonder* 108

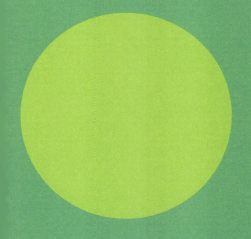

> WHEN YOU KNOW WHERE YOU WANT TO GO, AND YOU KNOW WHERE YOU ARE NOW, YOU CAN ALWAYS DO SOMETHING TO MOVE IN A BETTER DIRECTION.

SECTION 3.   FOUR CONVERSATIONS

Over the next 728 weeks of your child's life, some conversations may matter more than others.

> What you say, for example, regarding **pirates, spiders, and football** might have less impact on their future than what you say regarding **health, sex, technology, or faith.**

The next pages are about the conversations that matter most. On the left page is a destination—what you might want to be true in your kid's life 728 weeks from now. On the right page is a goal for conversations with your four-year-old and a few suggestions about what you might want to say.

Healthy Habits

Learning to strengthen my body through exercise, nutrition, and self-advocacy

This year you will <u>establish basic nutrition</u> so your child will have consistent care and experience a variety of food.

Maintain a good relationship with your pediatrician, and schedule a well visit at least once per year. You can also begin to build a foundation of healthy habits for your four-year-old with a few simple words.

SECTION 3.   HEALTH

Say things like...

> Let's pick a healthy snack.

> Can you help me cook?

> Thank you for trying that.

> I love to watch you run / ride / kick the ball!

> Did you know carrots grow underground?

> Will you throw the ball with me?

> Did you wash your hands?

Reflect

HINT:
Okay, "exercise" may be a stretch, but climbing and sliding and swinging count.

What are your goals for providing your four-year-old with good nutrition and exercise?

SECTION 3. HEALTH

What are some ways you might try to improve your four-year-old's nutrition? Do they eat vegetables and fruit regularly?

Parenting Your Four-Year-Old

Who will help you monitor and improve your four-year-old's health this year?

SECTION 3.   HEALTH

What are your own health goals for this year? How can you improve the habits in your own life—you know, even though sometimes Saturday "lunch" consists of leftover Goldfish® crackers?

Sexual Integrity

Guarding my potential for intimacy through appropriate boundaries and mutual respect

This year you will introduce them to their body so your child will discover their body and define privacy.

Your four-year-old may be so comfortable with their body they have no problem running outside in their birthday suit. That confidence is a good thing, but it's also a good time to start coaching them to understand privacy and personal boundaries.

SECTION 3.　　SEX

Say things like...

> Close the door when you go to the potty.

> Don't touch your private parts in public.

> It's polite to look away when someone is changing their clothes.

> Can you give your sister some space?

> Your penis / vagina / bottom / nipples are private, and we don't show them to people.

> If someone touches your private parts, come and tell me right away.

> Your friend might not want you to sit on his face.

> Sometimes the doctor might touch a private part to make sure you are healthy. It's okay when I'm with you.

> It's always okay to tell someone 'no' if you don't want them to touch you.

Reflect

When it comes to your child's sexuality, what do you hope is true for them 728 weeks from now?

SECTION 3. SEX

Are you and your spouse, or your child's other parent, on the same page when it comes to talking about sex with your child?

How might you work on a plan to communicate your hopes and expectations about sex through real-time conversations with your child?

Parenting Your Four-Year-Old

HINT:
They won't remember it all after one talk. It will take many talks— over time—to communicate what you want them to know.

Write down a few things you want to communicate to your four-year-old about their body, right now in this phase.

SECTION 3. SEX

Technological Responsibility

Leveraging the potential of online experiences to enhance my offline community and success

This year you will <u>enjoy the advantages</u> so your child will experience boundaries and have positive exposure.

One advantage to technology is being able to play online games with your four-year-old. One disadvantage is that your four-year-old may not be a very magnanimous loser (if you happen to win). Either way, it's definitely a good idea to have some conversations about technology this year.

SECTION 3. TECHNOLOGY

Say things like...

I'm texting Grandma to ask a question.

Talk openly about technology as you use it.

Let me see what you did.

Show interest in what they do with technology.

You need to ask before you use the computer

Know when they are on a device and what they are using it to do.

It's time for you to put the iPad away.

Set limits for screen time.

I put my phone away when we are eating so we can talk to each other.

Let me show you what a galaxy looks like.

Use technology to enhance your conversations.

103

Reflect

When it comes to your child's engagement with technology, what do you hope is true for them 728 weeks from now?

SECTION 3. TECHNOLOGY

What rules do you have for digital devices in your family? If you don't have any, what are two or three that you might want to set for your four-year-old?

What are your own personal values and disciplines when it comes to leveraging technology? Are there ways you want to improve your own savvy, skill, or responsibility in this area?

SECTION 3. TECHNOLOGY

Parenting Your Four-Year-Old

Authentic Faith

Trusting Jesus in a way that transforms how I love God, myself, and the rest of the world

This year you will incite wonder so your child will know God's love and meet God's family.

Your four-year-old has many questions. Some might be about creation, heaven, church, and the Bible… and some of their questions might already be hard to answer. Don't panic. Just like other topics, answer faith questions as simply as possible. If they need to ask more, they will.

SECTION 3.   FAITH

Say things like...

God made you. God loves you. Jesus wants to be your friend forever.

Was Daniel afraid when he was thrown into the lion's den?

Talk about what your preschooler learns at church.

"Do not be afraid, for the Lord your God is with you" (Joshua 1:9).

Are you scared? Let's talk to God about it.

Isn't that wonderful? Let's thank God for it.

Let's make cookies for our neighbors.

Prompt them to help.

109

Reflect

Who will help you develop your child's faith as they grow?

SECTION 3.　　FAITH

Is there a volunteer at your church who shows up consistently each week for your child? Do you attend a consistent service so your four-year-old knows who will greet them each week?

When it comes to your child's faith, what do you hope is true for them 728 weeks from now?

SECTION 3.   FAITH

What routines or habits do you have in your own life that are stretching your faith?

Rhythms and Responses

CUE TIMES *Building Daily Rhythms* 116
UNEXPECTED *Preparing for the Unexpected* 122
CRISIS *Navigating Crisis* 126

Parenting Your Four-Year-Old

The rhythm of your week will shape the values in your home.

Now that you have filled this book with dreams, ideas, and goals, it may seem as if you will never have time to get it all done. Actually, you have 728 weeks. And every week has potential.

The secret to making the most of this phase with your four-year-old is to take advantage of the time you already have. Create a rhythm to your weeks by leveraging these four times together.

SECTION 4.   CUE TIMES

Morning Time

Set the mood for the day. Smile. Greet them with words of love.

Drive Time

Reinforce simple ideas. Talk to your toddler and play music as you go.

Cuddle Time

Be personal. Spend one-on-one time that communicates love and affection.

Bath Time

Wind down together. Provide comfort as the day draws to a close.

Reflect

What seem to be your four-year-old's best times of the day?

SECTION 4. CUE TIMES

What are some of your favorite routines with your four-year-old?

Parenting Your Four-Year-Old

Write down any other thoughts or questions that you have about parenting your four-year-old.

SECTION 4.   CUE TIMES

Preparing for the Unexpected

SECTION 4.   UNEXPECTED

Parenting humans at any phase of life is filled with the unexpected.

No matter the age, sometimes the unexpected discoveries we make as parents may elicit fear, anger, or confusion as we try to guide our kid toward a positive future. It may even be something that is completely out of our control, like a medical diagnosis or a family tragedy. That's why it's best to create a response plan when you are clear and thoughtful.

So, take a few, deep breaths. Find a place where you feel safe and comfortable. If you need to walk away and come back to this at a later time, that's okay, too.

Download → parentcue.org/preparing

Parenting Your Four-Year-Old

Reflect

Every parent has what it takes to navigate challenges with their kids, but none of us can carry the weight alone.

HINT:
Think of someone with whom you feel safe enough to be completely honest about what is happening and what you are feeling.

If you were to discover something you weren't expecting in your kid's life, who would you be able to call?

_____
_____
_____
_____
_____
_____

How would you begin that conversation?

_____
_____
_____
_____
_____
_____
_____
_____
_____

SECTION 4.   UNEXPECTED

Every kid who is navigating challenging situations needs their parent's involvement. But a parent may not be the only influence they need.

If you were to discover something you weren't expecting, who else in your kid's life could you count on to walk with them through this experience?

HINT:
Think of someone who shares your values.

_____
_____
_____
_____
_____
_____

What might you want to go ahead and share with them about your kid and/or your family?

_____
_____
_____
_____
_____
_____
_____
_____

Parenting Your Four-Year-Old

Navigating Crisis

What is a crisis?

A crisis is any real or perceived threat to your child. And it's inevitable. Even though you are a great parent, you won't be able to protect your child from some pain during their preschool years. There is a wide range of events that classify as "crisis" ranging from temporary to long-term and from mild to severe.

How do you recognize it?

Just because your preschooler may not know how to talk about it doesn't mean they are unaffected. Watch for these three things:

① Are they regressing?

During a crisis, preschoolers will often try to take more control of their world by regressing in potty training, verbal skills, motor development, or behavior.

② How are they playing?

As your preschooler plays with toys, listen to the conversations the toys have with each other and watch how the toys treat each other.

③ What are they drawing?

Preschoolers may begin to draw what they are processing. Asking your child about their drawings will give you insight into their mind and heart.

How do you respond to it?

① Re-establish some routine.
Preschoolers love predictability. Talk to them about changes in their routine while reminding them what has stayed the same. Establish new expectations and a new routine.

② Play with them.
If you notice something in your child's play, join them. Thirty minutes of one-on-one play with your child establishes a meaningful connection, which helps them feel safe.

③ Make music.
Music is healing. It's multi-sensory, non-threatening, structured, personalized, fun, and accessible.

④ Respect their boundaries.
When offering affection, model and respect their boundaries by asking, "Would you like me to hold you?" "Do you want a hug?" Your preschooler may need a safe space alone to process their emotions first.

⑤ Answer their questions.
Listen first. Paraphrase their words to make sure you understand their question and concern. Then, give an honest answer in a calm, reassuring voice, using as few words as possible.

⑥ Take care of yourself.
When your preschooler is in crisis, you may be in crisis as well. Seek care. Find community. Take some personal time. This may be the best thing you can do to help your child.

⑦ Get outside help.
Consider if your preschooler is being hurt by someone, hurting others, or hurting themselves. Or if you are also hurting and not currently able to provide support.

What's Next: The Kindergarten Phase

SUMMARY *The Kindergarten Phase* 134
TIMELINE *The Preschool Phase* 136
NOTES *Write and Remember* 140

Parenting Your Four-Year-Old

In only 52 weeks you will rediscover your preschooler as a kindergartner.

One of the joys of parenting is the many surprises that greet you around every corner.

We can't prepare you for all the joys that await you in the next phase, but we can give you a glimpse of a few things that might help you anticipate what's coming.

SECTION 5. WHAT'S NEXT

The kindergarten phase may look like…

- Writing lunchbox notes
- First day of Kindergarten emotions
- The tooth fairy
- Unfiltered opinions about your appearance
- Bicycle rides
- A need for more attention
- Learning to read
- Rambling end of day recaps
- Early mornings getting ready for school

In not so many weeks you may discover an emerging kindergartner who is saying, **"Look at me!"**

Kindergarten

The phase when unfiltered words make you laugh, school drop-off makes you cry, and life becomes a stage where your kid shouts, *"Look at me!"*

SECTION 5.   SUMMARY

Get ready for memorable statements.
By this age, a child can speak in sentences… and long, wandering monologues. But you will be amazed and entertained by all the profound and uncensored things they say, like, "How did you get the wrinkles out of your hair?" and, "You're talking so much I can't hear you."

Adjust for a cultural shift—school.
This means less time for play, more early-morning alarm clocks, and a higher demand for focused attention. While kids at this age thrive on routine and predictability, they also crave opportunities to have a little unstructured play, a chance to skip and run, to throw and catch, and to use their imagination.

Give some undivided attention.
While previously a kid might have been one adorable toddler drawing the attention of multiple adults, they are now in a classroom with multiple kids—some even as cute and as smart as they are. At school, at church, or on the soccer field, one thing is true: They want your undivided attention. So give it as often as possible.

The Phase Timeline

HINT:
The full Phase Timeline is available at parentcue.org/timeline.

About the Timeline
The one thing that is true across every phase is that your child will change—and so will your role as a parent. The phase timeline is a visual to help you see the progression through their first 18 years. Reference it over time to remember where you have been and to get an idea of where you are heading.

About the Curve
Your child will also experience different levels of intensity across the phases. Watch for where the line rises to know when your child may be experiencing more developmental intensity. Whenever that seems overwhelming, this timeline is a reminder that it's just a phase.

Remember: We haven't met <u>your</u> kid. This timeline is just what's true for a lot of kids.

SECTION 5. TIMELINE

Preschool → Your role is to embrace their physical needs.

↓

Elementary School → Your role is to engage their interests.

↓

Middle School → Your role is to affirm their personal journey.

↓

High School → Your role is to mobilize their potential.

Parenting Your Four-Year-Old

The Preschool Phase

Your Role →

Embrace their physical needs.

Zero

One

Two

New Baby

Wants to know...
Am I safe?

So...
Establish trust.

One-Year-Old & Two-Year-Old

Wants to know...
Am I able?

So...
Develop their confidence.

SECTION 5.   TIMELINE

Thinks Like →

A preschooler thinks like an artist, so engage with their senses.

Motivated By →

A preschooler is motivated by safety, so respond consistently.

Three • **Four** • →

Three-Year-Old & Four-Year-Old

Wants to know...
Am I okay?

So...
Cultivate their self-control.

Parenting Your Four-Year-Old

It's just a phase, so don't miss it.

SECTION 5. NOTES

Parenting Your Four-Year-Old

SECTION 5. NOTES

Parenting Your Four-Year-Old

SECTION 5. NOTES

Parenting Your Four-Year-Old

SECTION 5. NOTES

Be the parent you want to be with Parent Cue.

We believe in every parent's ability to be the parent their child needs. Good parenting takes on many forms!

Parent Cue is here to cue you with what you need, when you need it—curated content, weekly inspiration, free resources, products, and more—so you are equipped to be the parent you want to be.

Get started → parentcue.org

PARENT CUE

Parent smarter, not harder.

Make the most of everyday moments on the go. Download the free Parent Cue app to get weekly cues and content to connect with your kid in every phase from New Baby to Twelfth Grade—available for iOS and Android. Weekly phase content also available with an in-app subscription.

Download now → parentcue.org/app

Parenting Your Four-Year-Old

Ready for the next phase.

These guides are the core product of the Phase Project—a synthesis of personal experience, academic research, and gatherings of leaders and educational experts from across the child development spectrum.

Just like this one, each guide will help you make the most of every phase in your child's life through:

① What is changing about your kid
② The six things your kid needs most
③ Four conversations to have each year
④ Rhythms and responses
⑤ What's next

PHASE GUIDES

A guide for every phase.

This guide is one of an eighteen-part series, so you can follow your parenting journey across every phase from New Baby to Twelfth Grade.

Preschool Phase

New Baby
The "I need you now" Phase

One-Year-Old
The "I can do it" Phase

Two-Year-Old
The "I can do it" Phase

Three-Year-Old
The "Why?" Phase

Four-Year-Old
The "Why?" Phase

Elementary School Phase

Kindergartner
The "Look at me!" Phase

First Grader
The "Look at me!" Phase

Second Grader
The "Sounds like fun!" Phase

Third Grader
The "Sounds like fun!" Phase

Fourth Grader
The "I've Got This" Phase

Fifth Grader
The "I've Got This" Phase

Middle School Phase

Sixth Grader
The "Who Cares" Phase

Seventh Grader
The "Who's Going?" Phase

Eighth Grader
The "Yeah… I Know" Phase

High School Phase

Ninth Grader
The "This is Me Now" Phase

Tenth Grader
The "Why not?" Phase

Eleventh Grader
The "Just Trust Me" Phase

Twelfth Grader
The "What's Next?" Phase

Shop now → phaseguides.com